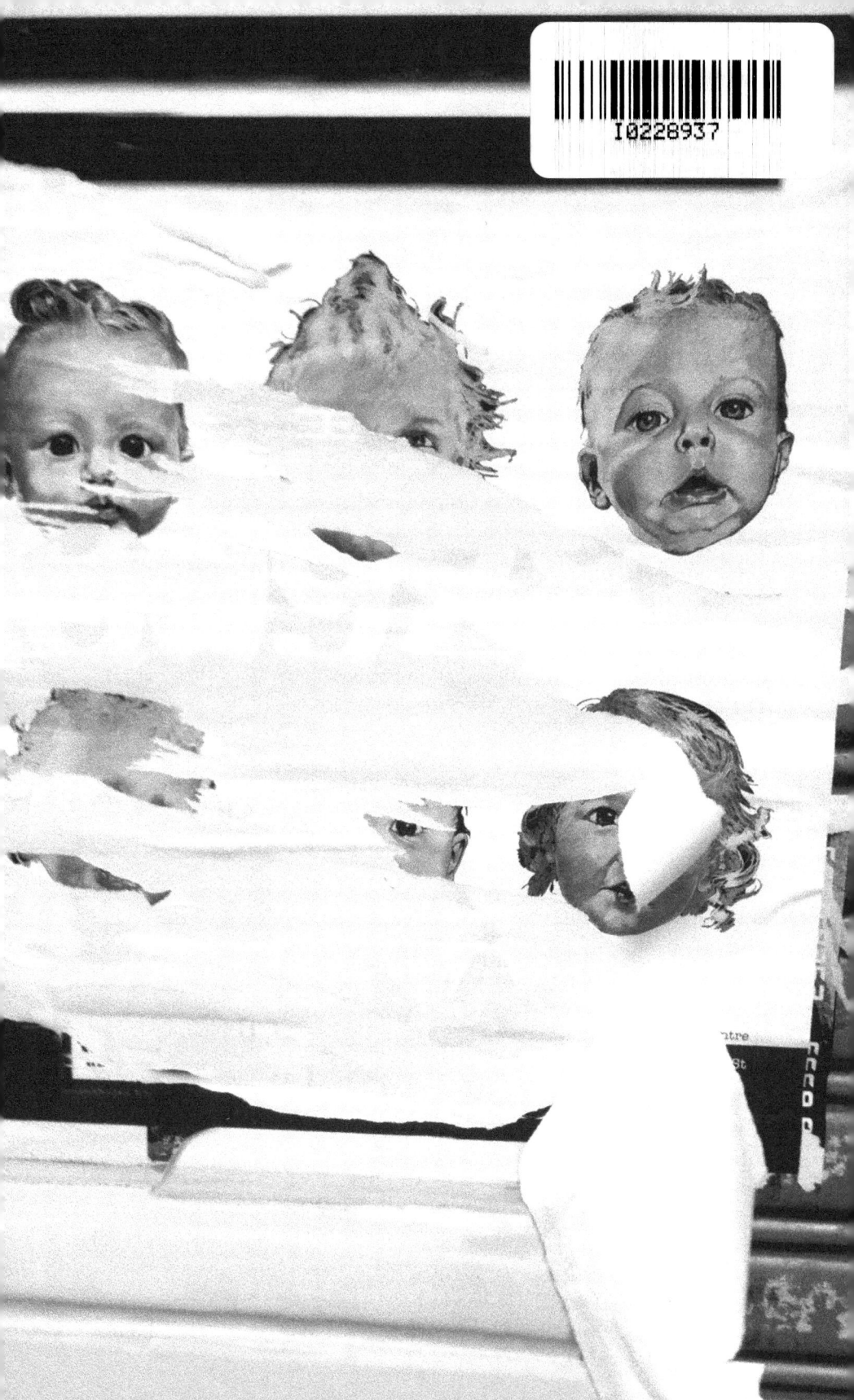

COPYRIGHTED MATERIAL

© 2015 copyright by Martin Nakell

First edition. All rights reserved.
ISBN: 978-0-9820775-0-4

Printed in the United States of America. No part of this book may be used or reproduced in any manner whatsoever without written permission from the publisher, except in the case of brief quotations embodied in critical articles and reviews. For information please email: questions@jadedibisproductions.com

Published by Jaded Ibis Press, an imprint of Jaded Ibis Productions, LLC, Seattle, Washington USA.

Cover design and art © by Debra Di Blasi.

UNNAMED:
THE EMOTIONS

new poetry by

Martin Nakell

Jaded Ibis Press
sustainable literature by digital means™
an imprint of Jaded Ibis Productions
Seattle • Hong Kong • Boston

TABLE OF CONTENTS

Dedication

Royal Palm   13

Cross   16

Polis Acropoliticum the Citizen of the Universal Humankind   21

Negombo 1   23

Negombo 2   24

Riverside   25

Horses Come Listlessly, of Course(s)   28

Trans/Pirate Inside the Universal Humankind   29

Formative   31

A Conversation Among – Iraq   32

Observations of Mt. Epomeo   33

A Physics as Heat   34

Ox   35

Comma Written in the Hand of the Universal Humankind   36

Historiography of a Landscape   38

From a Study on Rhythms   43

From a Study on Rhythms	44
A New York Times Its War About Universal Humankind	45
Rain Disquisition of Rain	47
Albert Einstein Write That...	52
Timbres Off Of The Universal Humankind	53
Her Youngest Daughter	55
Advent in Estate Place	56
Copia	57
A If Is At An	59
A Festivity of the Sound Image L	63
Again Asea Astride A Harvest	65
Because of Bobby Hutchinson Billy Childs Derek Oates	66
Coincidence Elements Discover the Universal Humankind	68
Thirty-One Questions to Ask Yourself While Looking in a Mirror	70
Begin Ascent of Universal Humankind	75
Further Adventures Ad Ischia	77
To Cross	80
Alives Forward Toward Universal Humankind	81
From a Study of the History of Languages	83

Con:verse	84
At Night Izzzz Dawn Iz	85
To Zleep of the Universal Humandkind	86
The Repetitions	89
A Concrete	90
Agribiz	93
Ice Cream	94
Fragmentation	95
Pandolce With the Universal Humankind	96
Mineral Chemical Arithmetical Humankind	97
About the Author	

for Rebecca

and for Noam Mor

and for Deanne Belinoff

Martin Nakell

ROYAL PALM

If the gate is open go through it

    If the gate seems to ask you a question don't answer it

        If the gate answers your question believe it

            If the gate is a woman listen to her

                If the gate shows anger be careful

                                            be very careful
                                            but keep on

                If the gate approaches you it is a false gate

                    If the gate is anywhere but here don't trust it

If the gate explodes don't forget it

    If the gate bears an inscription read it
        then read it again and at least once more

        If the gate is beautiful take delight

If a stingray flies through the opened gate wait to see what it looks like when it comes back. If it's still a stingray, go home. If it doesn't come back, don't go home. If the stingray was white and it returns particolored tolerate frustration until conflicting ideas open you with particolored poise

If the gate is blue, even if cobalt blue, or sea blue, or sky blue, or baby blue or navy blue go into town to join the Festival of Wellbeing

                If the gate is closed close the gate

If someone has jimmied the gate find them to study with them

    If someone has jimmied the gate, go through, find them, throw them out

UNNAMED: The Emotions

If this gate exists you can live

This gate exists

If this gate doesn't exist you can live

If you see posted on this gate a notice that a woman who feasted on a full kilogram and a half of scampi a fisherman kept bringing her died of scampi poisoning make a ballad of it and pass it along the seashore singing of how happily she died and of how happy her old husband was to see his young wife die happy on her husband's one hundred twelfth birthday

If the gate leads to somewhere you believed did not exist

then you can no longer believe yourself

If someone tells you the gate is not meant for you
tell them they better run the sea has caught fire and then swim through the gate

If you hear rumors about the gate collect them write them expand on them watch them contradict each other use the contradictions to expand them further

If you become afraid of the gate watch your fear as through a window

If the gate is simple take it for granted the way you must be taken by yourself If the gate is ajar just think about it don't worry

If the gate is made of scientific formulas consisting of numbers and/or other signs either fixed or floating then investigation convenes a history of potential vis a vis the difference between tasting and seeing

If the gate exists free-standing, without walls, in the middle of everywhere you have interesting options If the gate is a different gate every time you pass it, can you believe in essence? If the gate is the same gate every time you pass it can you construct a notion of passage that includes every part of your body that accounts for its physical characteristics including shape function biomagnetic electrical process and meaning and connect your body to everybody's body

If the gate seems like something to approach to touch then do that when you have fear balanced with a primitive urge heard about in contemporary music

If the gate becomes so familiar that you hardly notice it then it's possible you have begun the perpetual image-shifting process you had studied written about on a notice posted on the gate

CROSS

To cross this desert you need a hyrohoroscope

you need a winter hydropither

you need a floral magnemizer

to cross this desert

you need body ferminizer

you need a capacious arbolitage

you need a mind of desert

you need a pragmatical fibrocunculator

to cross this desert

you need a tautological eye

you need a friendship made of

transcontinental proportions

free of disease conversant

with the electrical impulses

causing doubt

to cross, to cross, to cross

you need a bag of desires

tied by a sailor slung

over your missing shoulder

to cross this desert you must

put an artificial foot in the sand

to absorb the shocks of distances and vertigoes

to cross this desert you must hide

the list of the women of childhood

beneath a rock as a marker you must piss there

to cross this desert you must subscribe to and read

the magazine called Bitterness & Grace

to cross this desert you must invent a god

you must invoke his name from an opened throat

until his name is synonymous with the verb to be

in its active tense

to cross this desert

you must calculate the difference

between the sun and the moon the distance

and circumference of each the

ratio between the square

root of moon and the parabola

of sun

to cross this desert

you must cross this desert

UNNAMED: The Emotions

perhaps you never will undertake the journey

look at where it got Moses

after all look at where it got

his people

but you're not like that

because already you have imagined yourself

in the garden be it

on the other side be it

stuck in the desert

be it of pruned cosmos

or dahlia be it of monsters

flora from a secret desert

cavern.

That's who you all are all of you

you see on your way

be they phantoms be they neighbors

offering the sustenance they expect

from you

to cross this desert, muster

the art of repetition

to cross this desert increase

Martin Nakell

day by day your intake of water

in inverse proportion to your intake of oxygen.

To cross this desert give someone

all the reckless excess terror

the world has manufactured for them to process

in a mechanical micropileator into ploughshares

or breath

To stand

on the desert's far side.

To have been waiting for you so long

To have exhausted 6,352 forms of sight.

They grow like weeds even here.

You wouldn't believe it.

I harvest them with my son's chapped hands.

Je t'embrace, Time whispers in the desert.

I will translate that into the white language

you will speak one day

a clean effulgent language

each word a neologism

freed of the future

of its illusion.

To cross this desert you need

UNNAMED: The Emotions

a pack-mule, a water-tank,

a hat, something for the eyes

& no compass because direction

doesn't matter, but you will need

a bifurcated circular ambivilator,

you will need a wooden

arrow on a stick to plant in the sand

once in a while

telling you "go this way" or "go back

that way."

Martin Nakell

POLIS ACROPOLITICUM OF THE
CITIZEN UNIVERSAL HUMANKIND

      your city floats.

      the man whose head emerges from the pavement has put his hat on the chair.

      the imp in your body

      and the imp in the body of your city

conspiring erase memory
and heaviness but knowing remains

      armies withdrawn to outside the eight gates city

      synapses painted on shields

      leaned up against quiet columns of air this is not surrealism

      look outside the window at the man

whose head rests on the pavement

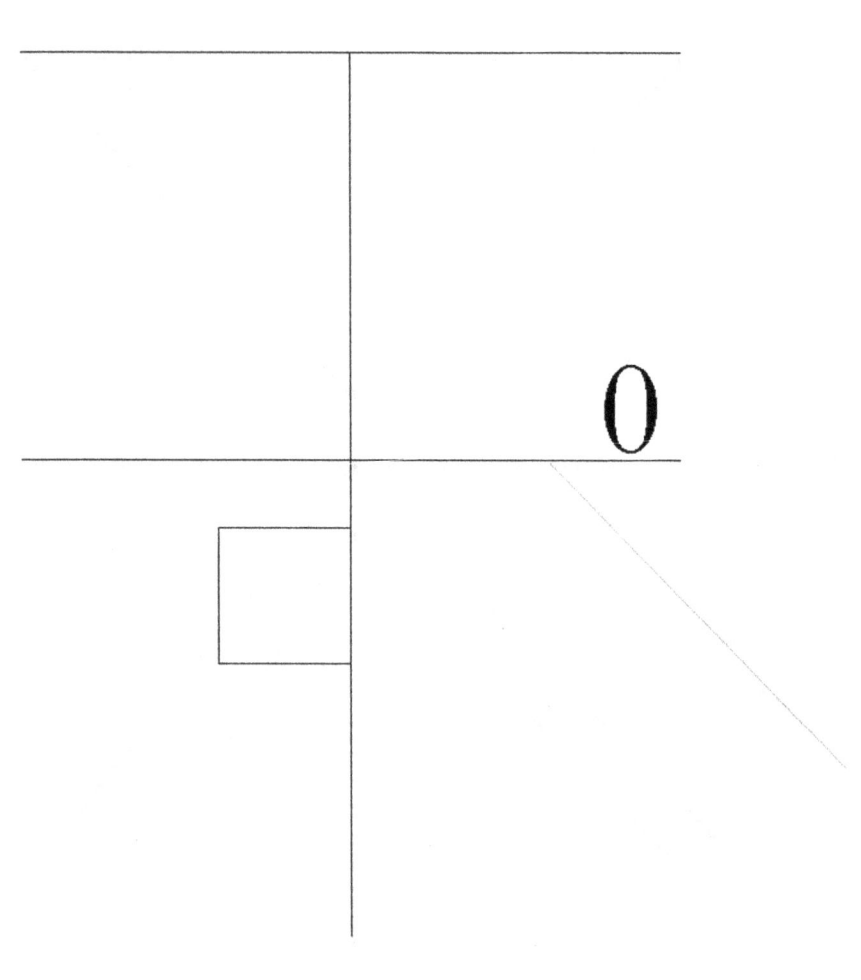

Martin Nakell

NEGOMBO 1

wall/stone
water/harnessed
word/water
water/power
light/heaviness
gravitas/lightness
sun/light/focused
children/babies little
girls/little boys
women stone/water
water/slowness
heaviness/balance
lifted/stone
labor/song
stone/float
poem/gather
sight/water
muscle/walk
sun/play
body/water
water/muscle
water/song
sun/water
sun/light/harnessed
heat/water
dream/birth
birth/water
water/solemn
knowledge/water
water/gate
song/dance
water/dance
it's-not-about-death/water
sleep/stone
breath/stone
Amen.

NEGOMBO 2

Bay of moon

white butterfly

mineral rust

temple of the godless

stele

fountain nest

the idea of water.

The relationship

between the eye and the navel.

Who walks out of the cave

into the cold.

A wall divides them

for the sake of clarity

When Ambience issues her warning

the body stimulates comfort

In the labyrinth

things become easier

the opposites draw closer

under the dome

vision inscribes concentric circles

light as breath

Martin Nakell

RIVERSIDE

As usual we were arriving by train but then just

Reading the post card where it said

or remembering the way you sat on the roof watching the wild parakeets, green, listening to their raw their

once it was like that, then again, again

what images repeated themselves: cones, the idea of cones; certain numbers embedded in certain structures; trees: as growth, as crosses, as shade; bodies of water: crossing them, delving, emerges from; horses; and on

wondering again about aesthetic principles but knowing that wasn't the issue then finding that it was

what did the primitive religions do? not before there were images before there was language but before, prior to

walking up and down the aisles for a while that was all right looking at them, families and

landscapes landscapes

there was one with a tree or the image of a tree and that's the only now way to think about a thing is to

this is not a

What was it you wanted that day, mostly? Had I given it to you? Looking back I

we had found something on the ground together, but I hadn't seen its value until he, well, he in his fingers he enframed holding it

up

they were anxious, sick with it, then they were ok again

forests of them

UNNAMED: The Emotions

their voices made you laugh, do you remember? I remem

passing the time there

just before we got there we were waiting yet listening to it was a music a drone chant a voice susurrating some wordzound like that some

as though there were some machine attached to their time which

distracted it while they/

      it was some kind of humming to it
while they

You collected yourself there and into what? Some fiction tale poem or other? that kept draining. that needed you to

they flew over the house they were green incredibly fast wild fulsome beating those wings they surprised you the way you had surprised things the way you had

as usual

kept arriving

through the tunnel out from among farmlands the river beside it
beside which it kept thinking while the river moving like a river like something it wasn't with us inside of it moving not knowing if we were or

whether the way you smiled at that what I saw in it then waiting to arrive and

and a river arising beside it and

you come down to tell me they were in the trees and did I

or had I what you needed was when I said yes it is?

the way it was black there not like a river yet a river and the
way everyone seemed unaware of it was remembered from dreams or walking, sitting there or looking up and down or the way it kept rising was black or

a thing like that isn't something to ignore. two of them
flying through green screeching it isn't only beauty I said no you

Martin Nakell

agreed it isn't a not only

nor something to ignore

there were images that kept repeating they were one thing and then

decisions are like that or arrivals sounds that recur or which way you are going you can tell by the river glancing at it through the window there beside

well beside

everything in that one

image all of

                      take the flame the image of it

    acknowledges that's what

it does

like a river does or the animals in the coming

the way you were up there

the way you were there up

as though that were the visual image you

as usual we were arriving

by train or leaving but then just after

HORSES COME LISTLESSLY, OF COURSE(S)

listlessly come Horses by fences neighing neighs and otherwords. Here come walking clouds in skies dropping leaflets. Horses, unable to read the leaflets, neighing, even braying, more and more and more loudly. Neighing fills the canyon. Horses to gallop by fences wording leaflets. Clouds in skies emptied of leaflets follow, also gallop. Wind blows hard. Horses run the other way, away from words, but clouds follow, until clouds fall, on, ride horses, until horses fall, now wordless, now neighless, rest, turn in tall grasses, horse-laughing, pissing, shaking, rising, falling, falling, arising. Oh, horses of your arms & legs, horses of your mouth your thigh horses of your histories horses of your thorough constant horses yet cloud horses to conjure horseness day by hour by languid by expanding epoch of horses. Childhorses, shy, listless, full of future neighs of ignorance & grasses, horse, by fencepole & fencepole unto perspective. you leave us speechless you cloud besmitten you. leave us as humankind we clap our hands we make that sound we listen to it to each other.

TRANS/PIRATE INSIDE THE UNIVERSAL HUMANKIND

he was born in the middle of a lake his first cousins were fishes were fishermen his first breath water. by the time he arrived on sandy sunswept rainpatient shores they were expecting they him met they with love with rage. day mingled with night creates a sustenance he tastes seeks words to describe flavor. closing eyes he takes in the first breath of air calling it body. he sleeps in the cradle of odors to distinguish wood from urine / nature from divine. knowing an alphabet awaits him that would formulate a passage from instinct to sign he can not foresee it. knowing he would stop but without cessation`n nowhere he prepares a vision of triangles circles parallelograms all interlocking layered harmonic and constant. knowing where to stop stands he there holds water in one hand the discovery of salt in the other

Martin Nakell

FORMATIVE

You have literally become a bird
          transformatively
These are not the same stairs they walked down
one year ago and why not?

Look at the birds at dawn. which one?
They all sleep.

These are the same stairs they walked down
one year ago and why not?

Every wall in the village bore the graffiti:

if you just calm down then there
is the world

        signed with a different name on each wall:

Karl Marx
Sigmund Freud
Charles Darwin
Ho Chi Minh
Jesus of Nazareth
Pontius Pilate

These are the same stairs they imagine
when imagination requires a light from a real world to burn
intelligence into sustenance

UNNAMED: The Emotions

A CONVERSATION AMONG – IRAQ TO AFGHANISTAN

To awaken to find oneself here without learning how to get here

To learn so suddenly the meaning of a word heretofore only analogized

To speak among us ourselves for the value to valuing

To fear that what we might say has been already been said but not about our but to cross that t for god's sake that xyz

To turn to keep turning so the eye in motion in case of appearance

To know that not knowing was a way of absolving

I keep asking what had you dreamt last night inside the night before in order to see

You who are with me who am with you might we be gods at a witches' Sabbath are we

To wallow together or there some other naming ceremony to attend to

Talking to gather speech because the hands are copious among us

What happened before speech was a silence in the making

Listen to the sounds explode around us a symphony of human desire

If we introduce ourselves to each other a book will be born

If we write a note each to pass to the other then the animals will rehearse with us a transition into the human

Let's each one of us in turn tell the tale of our youth in order to become one such tale filled with the figures of chance as an opulence

When we each one of us return let's each carry a leaf a stone a shard off a planet from outside our galaxy then engage in a discourse concerning whether sight or touch is the proper path to the soul and as to get here again from where as what is danger

OBSERVATIONS OF MT. EPOMEO

She wears the black hat as if it were a peach

She speaks in that her voice are made of glass

She looks at the landscape around her an animal constantly changes species

She listens to everyone else what they have to say in that each one of them resides mostly in relation

She comes to the table bringing photographs of the future to present to the diners as if laughter only took the form of prophecy

She curses only those who wear amulets of stone sewn into their own eyes

She sleeps in the bedroom that once belonged to the stranger she had rescued from obscurity with a continuous stream of translations from a continuous stream of obscurities as if there was only one continuous night on earth in which to embrace

She steps lightly sometimes out of fear sometimes out of caution sometimes out of her awareness that with each step the ground pushes up on her as if she could float away

She harnesses all the forces of the political world to claim victory over victory

She rises from defeats willing to enjoy the bread that had never been an object of sacrifice or adoration

A PHYSICS AS HEAT

Turtles camel for the sun to speech :

        in a slow drip up –

                ward

    water evaporates

You are not afraid of your fear to put your hand on the woman's breast

    Or remember the newspaper announcement

        of your first ejaculation in a small town on the banks of a great

    mass of water

    Or touching the altar after the doors had spread open in that darkness

Men eat ceremoniously
    spending imaginations
even if dining on regrets and the sublime
        or even the beautiful

        Don't let them frighten you!

The music has begun to beginning

    everyone labored long labored hard

    on instruments where did
        they learn this how

did they know the tablecloth

THE WORLD NOW IS CALM FOR WALKING

Martin Nakell

OX

ox flute ax man man
ahchs man ox flute float
man ox wound float
woman flute space air cut
ox ax eat flute heart float
slute space mind flesh dirt
sound

oaks nerve draw man man
blood spindle twice round
wash clean come tone song
clap loud clap clap
woman woman lean body toward
death fall light pound
ahchs   man ox wound float
blade

bend lift ax woman woman
pulse bind wrap clench
tooth ox blend burst wait
hold take lift life ochs
burst blood ox drip
dirt sand teeth
grit bite crust burst
beat blade sound slice
hold clench vein spine tingle

cra craw clo drah
sta breh blow
dow koo trum
sleet srade draw blow
sum iaum toke

toke toke
sloy man man

COMMA WRITTEN IN THE HAND OF THE UNIVERSAL HUMANKIND

At long last after centuries of debate you are alone with the geometry of sunflower whose leaves emerge green of course from its stem dense to take a more narrow more pointed form than its yellow petals that surround its brown corona that encircles its black epicenter

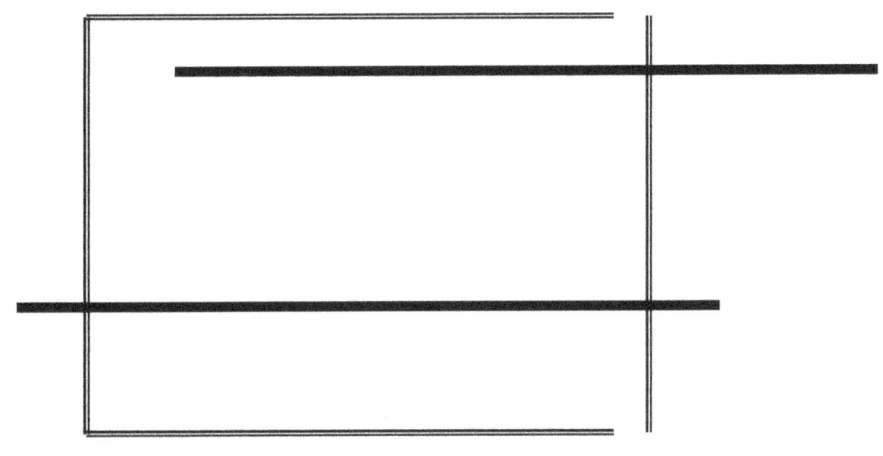

UNNAMED: The Emotions

HISTORIOGRAPHY OF A LANDSCAPE

From where does the myth of absence? is it only singular or can there be plural? Is there a balancing act that love requires of mythos?

and also a poetry of repose. where nipples. Of time spent indivisibly — without value, of an endless supply

When she stood on the roof to see the day and count the birds, he called to her. What was said? that later, when she asked him, as he declined to repeat it, his disaffirmation was what opened to the distance she had been looking

Is it possible to imagine a city without memories of a city? There's a solid brick building, a high school where for many of them begins a trajectory of images strung together whose each face bears the image of an ancestor. There, a lawn where conundrum poured directly out of nightmare. There's the exact hill where, looking out at the lights of the city they proposed that lights were an image of light. They proposed that what they saw they could become. There's the couch where a father slept. There's the direction through streets where, walking daily, it would be possible to learn the process to separate denial from solitude. Here is the bakery where she sent her messenger Sunday mornings. Here are the stairs which posed to them the question of whether it mattered if eventually one went up or one went down.

She is traveling in Asia. She is learning languages that they also speak in many of the districts of his city. In her pocket she carries one from a pair of dice. He doesn't carry the other. Purposefully, they lost it together. Once they concluded there were events that occur before languages. Because he feels them as they leave her body after one more turn of their die

There are things to be said to each city. Each thing must be said at a certain place. There is a kitchen where someone sat once beside a yellow refrigerator talking to a friend while she cooked. There is a room where music was made until the music so surprised them that they kept going until they came to an end they hadn't imagined. Then they left, laughing at the skills they hadn't recognized in their technique. There is a cemetery where someone's grandfather buried his confusions. Everyone who still wants to discuss them with him makes pilgrimage. Yet the room where he was born is far away. Distance creates irrealities which must be resolved. Each thing must be said at a certain place. Each word pronounced in a certain order. Then your it will open. A calm pulse beneath its nerves.

A man talks about the celibacy in his marriage. Then it will open. A persistent blue.

They had talked about their coming separation. When he noticed her eyes he took them for the eyes of someone whose name he couldn't remember. She will think that she sees that person in various parts of Asia. When she comes back she will say that there was something yet to complete about her trip

a poetry which is itself without value of an endless supply

She asks questions about his sexual past, about what he would or wouldn't do. These interrogations are like narratives. Strung together they reveal a plot. There is a motive. There is no crime. Neither he nor she are going to kill, yet in this novel there will be a living body, and it will be washed up not at the literal edge of their ocean, but washed up nonetheless, born by water, even if it surfaces beneath suguaro in their desert.

Levels of stress had increased for residents of the city. There were many reasons, all of them interwoven into a complex pattern plottable by discerning the movements of each resident on any given day, then computing the plot of those movements with a certain mathematical formula. She recited that formula to him, and he took its meanderings for a recitation of her desire never to cease their conversations

UNNAMED: The Emotions

It had become essential to abandon guilt as a strategy. It had become essential to abandon oneself to guilt as a strategy. Was it possible to abandon strategy, or was that an urgency found among the discovered manuscripts they were translating to re-read? How to abandon strategy? These were the x's manuscripts. When he died in this same city where he now lives, he left them behind, with nothing to help understand them except the letters he had written to his favorite brother. They hadn't yet been able to find the letters but they were still looking through all the artifacts

In all the letters she sent him the ink ran out exhausted itself before she got to a signature. He could hear her laughter in them, even though he knew there were difficult days there, when the foreign languages suddenly made no sense the local food inedible. They had abandoned themselves to both innocent and demonic laughter while around them the air fell to the ground leaving a space in which to enter other lives they would initially designate as foreign

Different political systems arise from different histories. There is much about each one's present history that another will never know. There are certain words gestures agreements which make all

history present in the moment and new. It's impossible to walk in any city without being aware of the politics of a thousand years. It is impossible to purchase a meal without consenting to the politics of the moment. It is impossible to give a gift unaware of its implications. A few of them carry the Mayor's phone number. Others have biographies of the Chief of the Border Guards. Most of them know what streets to avoid at what times of day. We will never need to discover the absolute origin of our species.

In all the letters she sent, she never mentioned him, she never mentioned herself. She described the places she visited precisely, with magnifying detail. He was left with a series of images that he rearranged, alternating her descriptions with images of objects he had seen in his own city.

describes a woman who walks back and forth on one street, trying to capture everything on that street in her mind, from the large black letters on the laundry, to the man eating in the restaurant window, to the peregrinations of a doorman. Because I have nothing, she thinks. Her street is in Hong Kong, in Saigon, in Kyoto, in Detroit, pronounced Day-trwah.

He had said that he couldn't bind her to him. Did she know what he was also thinking, as he said that? Computers make it even more evident that we don't possess our money, now that our money is electronic blips on a screen that float across a grammar of commerce. Did he know what she was also thinking as she heard that? They, who are all balanced between reason and something else. One of them read on the subway, standing, holding the strap, Maimonides, his Guide to the Perplexed.

Because she had been gone a long time he began a series of letters to her. Because he had to begin writing because he had little to say because of her absence he invented a language. The end of discourse is not silence. The means is mutability. The cause is [always] open to reinterpretation. The language of politics is audible through the voices of the dead. Having addressed all the envelopes to her in his invented language he was surprised that they got through. He had invented so many names for her.

Since there is no way to avoid avoidance of fate. Exhaustion. No one has come to harm you. One of them lays their head down in a map of the earth. By osmosis, cities, forests, mountains, seas, plains take shape where it matters. Money is abundant. Bridges build themselves as organisms, growing. Synapses are connectives across which electronic meaning flutters. A poetics that displaces a poetics of time precedes a poetics of spaces.

As she read the letters he sent her the technologies of distance became clear. It was then she knew that it's possible to go on traveling as if by mistake without return. Such mistakes have been made.

Each city has records of them. Reading those records you discover a way to correspond not with time but only space.

UNNAMED: The Emotions

Absence is an occurrence in the midst of. There was an elation. The mayor had been mayor for over forty years. Moved out here from New York, planning to go back. When he was working the night shift they visited the abandoned jail. The cells were tiny. There was little headroom. They went where the narrow spiral staircase had created a famous stabbing alley. They left by a back way through a metal door walking down seven flights of stairs.

To return to what he'd been saying the story he was telling them was changed by the discussion occasioned by the interruption. He who didn't recognize the new story went on telling it in the first person.

A poetics that proceeds to a poetics of spaces

Martin Nakell

FROM A STUDY ON RHYTHMS

staccato:

    the wind had become invisible

the show horse gallops across furious lawn

FROM A STUDY ON RHYTHMS

/ U /

    u / / / u / / / u

u / / / / u / / / /

Martin Nakell

A NEW YORK TIMES ITS WAR ABOUT UNIVERSAL HUMANKIND

Biggest punishing prized crucial smoldering ruling tightest absolute heaviest important grandest main key huge relentlessly harsh symbolic huge blunt severely uninhabitable unrepairable heavy rocket-propelled senior intensive mobile several missile six extraordinary assault prominent unsettling significant lasting security surveillance hidden chemical card nerve bloody gaping promised easy open unsearched subway recent terror carefully

Martin Nakell

RAIN A DISQUISITION OF RAIN

that rain which is eternity's eternal ice

that rain which announces the liberty of the unknown

the exquisite recreation of the singing of voyages he has taken that rain which returns after a brief hiatus bringing with it

its most voluptuous wind to sway trees upon whose bark rain sucks soaks that rain which returns after a million year absence

that rain which flows out streaming from your pores

that rain in which friendship becomes chatty

that rain my god in whose waters one's ancestors finally bathe enfin stretch out their bodies strained with the tensions they met that rain which wouldn't come and wouldn't come and at last that rain in which the child said my teacher said we would have

a great drought this year how can it be how can that rain be

that rain which causes predictable meditations in those who do not have to tremble in its cold

that rain which comes only once is annunciation

but not of a birth not of a salvation not of a miracle

that rain which announces hunger from the belly of its fall that rain, ravaging, which renounces anguish

which appeals to nourishment relishes comfort which expands to enlarge a universe of the acceptable

that rain which would not come for prayer nor dance nor to stop an imprecation

that rain which forced sight to the limit of the objective world which would

UNNAMED: The Emotions

imply nothing beyond it

that rain whose ax cut the cord at the astonishment of gasps

that rain which promised to return but never in a future

that rain which has no relation no brother no sister no mother and whose father is not crying but has stopped crying

that rain which turns day to the relief of dimness but turns darkness to something cubic that rain raining, suspended, pendulant, hanging

that rain from which there is no running, no flight, because direction is the first thing it laughs at that rain which we listen to, lying inside, all night, all morning, appeased

that rain which resolves the conversation between mr sublime and ms beauty while yet perpetuating it for the sake of something significant to do after the rain

that rain which stitches together the edges of leaf and air

that rain which proved the disexistence of God which sent the theologians scurrying for a topic to occupy the void for a rooftop which opened up a field of awe

that rain which refuses to command anyone to anything which issues grants to inertia that rain without metaphor that rain without syntax that rain without intention

the lawlessness of that rain remaking its own shape to remake the air's memory

the artfulness of that rain simultaneously remaking its own image

the betrayal of that rain promising nothing beyond the potential for rain that rain which pours out of our bodies in rituals we return to return

that rain which everyone even everywhere knows so that you might write to them about it that rain through which people have gone even so and nearly dauntless or in defiance

that rain which the gods did not ordain which surprised them that rain which the meteorologist predicts each night at sunset that rain which as a child said is nothing but rain

that rain which the rabbis discussed their words become magenta

that rain which affirms its position as the soul of denial which repeats yes yes that rain which sempeternally causes indicates announces signals motivates stasis that rain which drenched our ancestors' sleep

that rain which has quenched thirsts

that rain which the animals have aspired to imitate

that rain which will not provide the scholars with definitions but with permits

that rain which would provide the scholars with their definitions were they only willing that rain in which tedium flaunted its body

that rainsound resonant inimitable suggestible by certain sets of collected alphabetic symbols: tink, tick, tuck, tunk tong bing rit to annunciate the worlds of tin,,,,, concrete,,,,, roof,,,,, wood,,,,windowglass,,,,

that rain which kept track of the hours of the Creation and repeats them

that rain which adapts each molecule to the rapid changes of environment

that rain which infiltrates wisdom, spies on it, reports on it to itself which is its own superior that rain which drowned the men at war in the oath of their poem

that rain which did not flood but ran off the edges of earth whose source is perhaps exhaustible because the exhaustible and the eternal are equal

that rain which muted the world of the flora that rain which drowned workers at the frenzy of their piece-work benches

that rain which turned off the music of the spheres ah that

rain which made the distance between lost and lost unconditional that rain

which recaptured the sound of the Sermon on the Mount from where it had drifted off into space which recaptured the sound of Solomon making love to his people which recaptured that rain which giggles

that rain which disagrees with the proposition that the middle class is what drives

American prosperity

that rain whose migraine won't quit

that rain which the industrial revolution tried to abolish to displace to co-opt to find

a good use for that rain which produces an as yet unheard of and as yet unusable hydroelectric power

that rain which institutes reality by virtue of touch

that rain which had seen the face of God at Mt. Sinai which had not died that rain in which the homeless pursue their invention

that rain whose coming is a present of the act

that rain which Sappho drank into the corpus of her rhythm, ak-sensual that rain which stubbed its toe on a book

that rain which lacks all imagination

that rain with its base obsession compulsive repetition that rain in redictation to the form of rain

that rain which is round to be held in the palm of an emergency hand

that rain which directs eros in the performance of her pantomime, silent, daring, darling of the sages that rain whose exhaustion is velvet, whose violence bemuses the animal world

that rain which criticized no one, never knew sin, raged, never envied

that rain which anointed weariness with irony, fell on the heads of those who came pronouncing legends of floods

that rain which adapts each molecule to the millennial changes of environment that rain which incubates centuries until they are ready for profligate mortality

that rain which daedal mists all space fills in connects stands still moves rises as in falling

that rain a continuation of that rain which replies factually at the interstice of not becoming that rain which constitutes color mask formal setting ceremonial dress proper greeting

that rain which fixes their paint to their painted bodies that rain which insists on being written

that rain which creates destruction

that rain which analyzes the hypothesis of the discourse of absolute opposition that rain which concentrates being into clarity, transparency, density

that rain which autographs the flood of childhood at the soft speech of everyday sweat

ALBERT EINSTEIN WRITE THAT...

…the sun is a bird that invents the speed of light at the moment Adam & Eve hand in hand in hand in hand cross the threshold of a tangled garden Orpheyous calls Paradise which occurs now in a present which is also a forever the brain of that bird is the matter of the universe whose identity rises before it falls on the breath on the blinking of a wing whose motion describes an arc similar to the opening before the closing before the opening of an eyelid to swallow digest piss out light through the pores of the sweating human being in the heat of a day who rides astride the arc-back of a giant bird into the Psyche Suns & Explosions on Earth

Martin Nakell

TIMBRES OFF OF THE UNIVERSAL HUMANKIND

then does attempt forthright belonging then belonging then forthright then deer belonging then forthright belonging deer comfort attempt belonging attempt simplicity attempt deer attempt simplicity belonging notation forthright deer forthright belonging attempt scroll simplicity deer notation belonging simplicity attempt then simplicity belonging deer deer attempt fall attempt simplicity forthright notation simplicity scroll then scroll remorse attempt forthright belonging then deer simplicity authentic other does fall forthright authentic other belonging deer notation simplicity notation forthright other deer forthright remorse forthright belonging simplicity authentic attempt belonging other simplicity notation authentic forthright then deer deer comfort attempt notation forthright then deer telephone authentic scroll sail

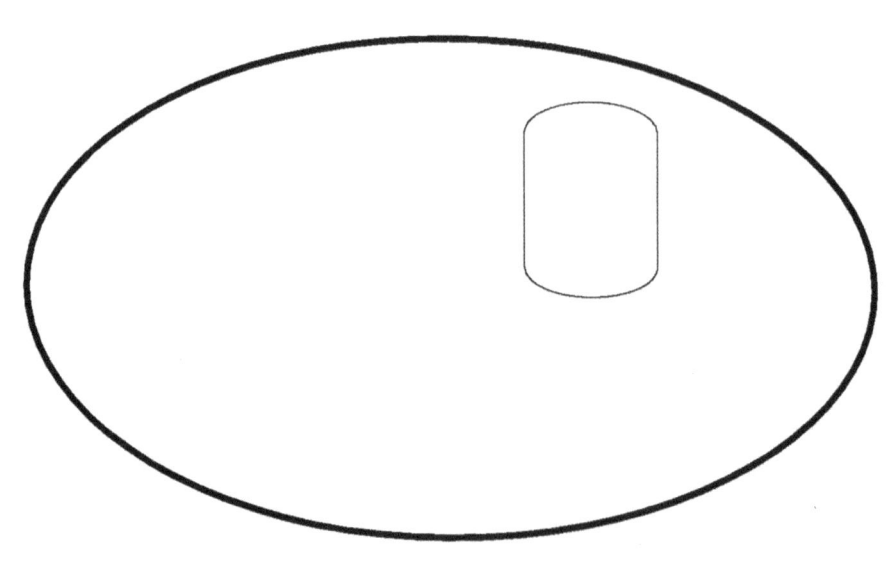

Martin Nakell

HER YOUNGEST DAUGHTER

Where is a landscape for these discussions I know I once saw it as a macaw flew 'twixt us with a birthstone in its breast you had turned my attention eastward it flickered that scapeland oasis in october with a crystal wind white threaded through the grasp you held on the bird's one feather. Flight, you had said to me then attempting a discourse of the absolute obvious can either delay or upsurge significance. Ever thing stands in way. We walk off together hand in body cleansed of Nothing negotiating a direction to beginning. When I walk by the edge of the cliff you hold onto me but we cannot not move from there we remain in hilarious stasis. Laughing lightly, languidly had we pronounced the word indifference. Smiling a prosody passed through our bodies unspoken although its echo clear in the valley. Remember that when I let go we obey the laws of motion space pleasure night.

ADVENT IN ESTATE PLACE

trees there didn't exaggerate
    after the long elevations you had been allowed to become human
if and only if then
    you would know what's good
        in taste
    & how to behave
        even the vine hadn't lied
          as as even as
    the group of women
        around the table
in the arbor
    discuss the methods
        to desacralize them selves
    a wind
        nor a birdchirp
neither disturb that sleep nor its anchor

COPIA

       in our three dimensional world

           poem signifies

              significance

because silence does not

    depend

  on language

          even though

              the color gold

                  depends

         on the color green

the space

     of time

is the aptitude

     of quality

the one wandering the nightest rooms

            artwalls   airlight   the release of question in beauty

   writes the commonest

      airletter illumination

         in the explosion of

UNNAMED: The Emotions

a newborn baby sitting at her breakfast reads an article in the newspaper about a newborn baby born comprehending an adult vocabulary but the newborn baby can't tell her parents about it then the wife asks the husband do you still love me and the husband says yes it's a mystery to me but even more so

Martin Nakell

A IF IS AT AN BY THE UNIVERSAL

"You exist" is true if and only if you exist

   "You are happy" is true if and only if you are happy

      "You are human" is true if and only if you are human

         "You are a poet" is true if and only if you are a poet

            "She is a mythologist who researches the origins of consciousness"
is true if and only if the ship Titanic sank at 41'46" N 50 '14" W on the night and morning of April 14 – 15 1912

"Goethe wrote the poem 'Peace Above All the Mountaintops' under a big beautiful tree which the German Nazis preserved, not cutting it down, but building their concentration camp around it" is true if and only if Goethe wrote the poem "Peace Above All the Mountaintops" under a big beautiful tree which the German Nazis preserved, not cutting it down, but building their concentration camp around it

   "Ciro loves Pina" is true if and only if when as Ciro loves Pina

"Odysseus had to wander the Mediterranean for 10 years after the fall of Troy because he angered Poseidon" is true if and only if Odysseus had to wander the Mediterranean for 10 years after the fall of Troy because he angered Poseidon

"The Mediterranean is a sea" is true if and only if the Mediterranean is a sea

"The child squatted in the shade eating his sandwich, raising it every three or four bites to his nose to smell the cooked meat, then, when he had finished eating, sang quietly to himself" is true if and only if the child squatted in the shade eating his sandwich, raising it every three or four bites to his nose to smell the cooked meat, then, when he had finished eating, sang quietly to himself

"Ten years pass during the time of ten years" is true if and only if ten years pass during the time of ten years

"The color green is red" is true if and only if the color green is red

"Human consciousness cannot comprehend death" is true if and only if human consciousness cannot comprehend death

"If and only if humankind invents language can logic create the condition of 'if and only if'" is true if and only if if and only if humankind invents language if can logic create the condition of if and only if

"Human consciousness cannot comprehend death; therefore people think of death with fear, drama, an enlivened urge to life, sorrow, stories & tales of an afterlife, scientific inquiry designed to discover something now secret still unknown about the universe that will make death comprehendible, release, reunion, rebirth, joy, indifference, despair, love" is true if and only if human consciousness cannot

comprehend death; therefore people think of death with fear, drama, an enlivened urge to life, sorrow, stories & tales of an afterlife, scientific inquiry designed to discover something now secret still unknown about the universe that will make death comprehendible, release, reunion, rebirth, joy, indifference, despair, love

"If and only if because" is true if and only if if and only if be cause

"If is if if is only is is if and if if if if if is only is" is true if and only if if is if if is only is is if and if if if if if is only is

"You had become an angel who danced the dance 'The Joyus of the Human

Body' at the Feast of the Noblest Gods on the far plain reveling in the Approval of the Grandmothers" if and only if the door is open and you have gone through it

"The physicist Paperno Franco declared in Rome that the problem time causes in discovering a Unified Theory is not that time, both particle and wave, cannot be resolved vis a vis gravity, but that time – passing both quickly and slowly while being also immediate – cannot be resolved vis a vis the laughter of animals" is true if and only if the physicist Paperno, Franco declared in Rome that the problem time causes in discovering a Unified Theory is not that time, both particle and wave, cannot be resolved vis a vis gravity, but that time – passing both quickly and slowly while being also immediate – cannot be resolved vis a vis the laughter of animals

"Almost finished reading this poem you vow to read poetry as often as possible because only poetry can explain to you in its inexplicable way that only poetry cannot explain without an explanation your life to you and it is that ability which gives birth to the words if and truth and you know that is what you are after is that is life to see no to feel those two words if and truth collide" is true if and and also if

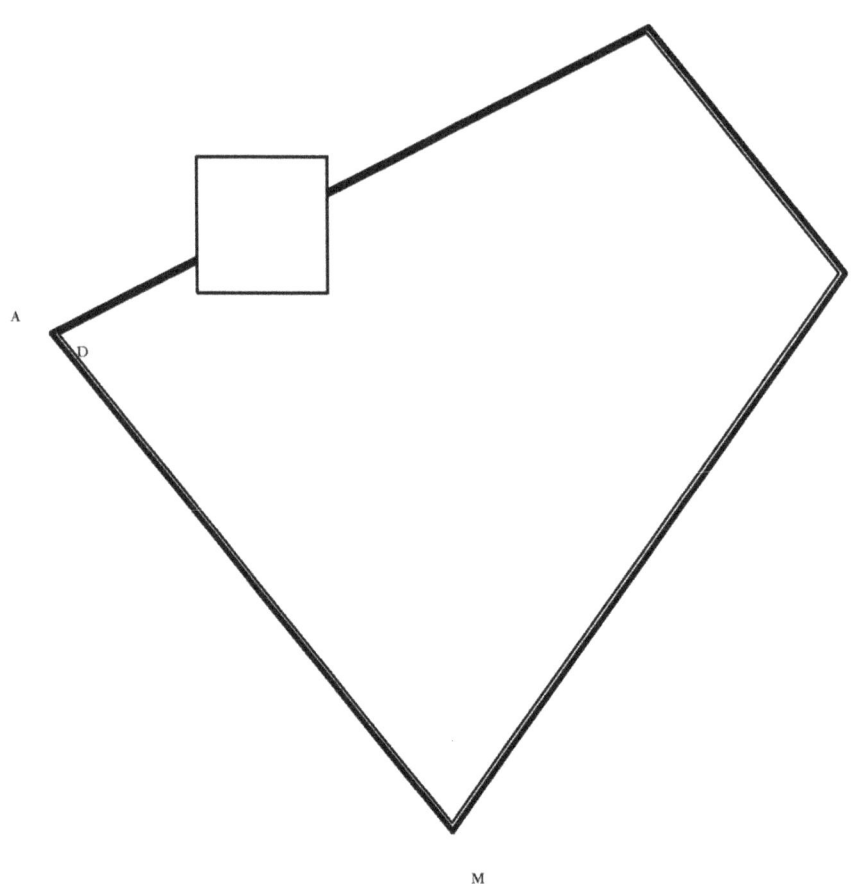

Martin Nakell

A FESTIVITY OF THE SOUND IMAGE L

Because of Jasper Johns

The word gray absorbs your attention no thought back into a universe
refractory

In a repository of stored personal possessions among things
      the mind knows twice time to repeat
      difference as sameness boundaries at distance

A museum guard watches a watcher who in that moment
                                    watches a painting
          in consideration of whether existence does not and integrate
               in these moments moments of the divine i.e. what
               or is or neither

In a forty-second dimension we see acumen abandon meaning for gaze
          the object ever seen
          the image remain

Water freezes pages
      youth appears tension sets
    vectors into energy spheres measure in precision
              with incision the increments designed to inscribe
          perfected long arcs suspended in open guests

I have been a farmer
I have been a thief
I have caught a trapeze using neither hand
nor eye I have ungrasped I have standed
          on the pavement
      to hear the drums from the fifth story window above
                    I have knocked on the door
      I have as fa

UNNAMED: The Emotions

When you have read
        the newspaper
           cover to
                  cover find some other
    use for an it.
Racing thoughts at the finished gate.
        Before he was aware of the idea he described an it of it

In a locus of anxiety a monochrome pulse gives birth to freedmen

                why war? freud wrote to einstein having
                meant to write about sphere
                    why detract from traditions why
                create a new

a wind, strip, a temperature, steep, a cosmography within a brain

                a quiet a sound a meaning among meetings
                devoid of distractions

  so that gray grew into growgrey say over over say over
        to remain steady grey expands into trace avoidavoid performs it
      self a wind a temp a peace defeared almost ideaform physical
      choice
    to move o'ward with it into what depth said contains it everybody is
    here now
  however they got here however they might remain however they are take
  memo of them
speechless note taker arriver ever river down

shut out once
    a vow to return
  grey informs greynessest graying at gray reaction it can be because harshness
  so demands it
                            stand up here upwise
    pronounced like a word was pronounced common secret that you are

AGAIN ASEA ASTRIDE A HARVES

again, always an am. last left. arms something sir thought asked away down poor love street. water behind. father men hear right come. lord man going bit black came course day door ever eyes face fellow first get girl give go god good got hand hat head himself house john know let life little long look might mother mr mulligan must name new night now old own place put round said saw says see still take tell thing think though three time told took two voice want went white wife without woman words world years yes young

UNNAMED: The Emotions

BECAUSE OF BOBBY HUTCHINSON BILLY CHILDS DEREK OATES & FOR REBECCA AG

in the continuing composition no term is interchangeable with another

Piano ≠ spiral

                                   Bass ≠ isosceles triangle

               Drums ≠ column

     Piano = circle

                                   Drums ≠ square

               Drums = depth

                                   Bass ≠ oblong

    Piano ≥ parallelogram

                       Drums ≠ cube

                                                          Piano ≤ unparallel lines

   Bass ≠ plane

              Piano ++ direction

                       Drums ≠ dimension
             Piano Drums

Bass ≠ elevation

Martin Nakell

　　　　　　　　　Bass √ circumference
　　　　　　　　　　Piano ∂ radius
　　　　　　　　　　Drums ≠ Bass
　　　　　　　　Piano 7r width

　　　　　　Bass ≠ orb

　　　　　　　　　　　　　　　　Drums ≠ octahedron

　　　Piano ≠ triangular prism

drums = trapezium

　　　　drums + oval

　　　　　　　　piano (((heptagon

bass *ellipsoid
　　　piano ≠ cylinder

　　　　　　　　　　　　bass ?'quadrilateral pyramid
　　drums ≠ sphere

　　　　　　bass ^ parallelepiped

drums ≠ truncated cone

　　　　　　　　　　　bass ≠ scalene triangle

piano --: hexagon

　　　　　　bass ≠ septagon

　　　　　　　　　　　　piano - kite

　　drums ≠ rhombus

　　　　　　　　　　　　piano ≠ dodechahedron
　　　　　　　　　　　　piano % icosahedron
　　　　　　　　　　　　bass ð romboide
　　　　　　　　　　　　bass　≠　　parallax

drum 8 drum　　　bass ≠ inscribed circle　　bass L. concentric circle

UNNAMED: The Emotions

COINCIDENCE ELEMENTS DISCOVER THE UNIVERSAL HUMANKIND

in the moment of danger an other other arrives

    rising from water with the words yes and was written on palm leaves

    one in each hand

the rabbi's word as it falls from studied lips becomes progeny who scurry

        singing that a happiness carries them over

    even the rivers of surfeit even of art

by the seawall

    the priest drunken mouths the names of a lover as sleep

        sleeps in the siesta heat should sleep's
        heart not also heal

    last night he dined quietly on only one poem late

        Tomatoes, her nerves were ardent they were green
        vines

of tomatoes she became a farm

        on the hill that farm that in fame raised navigations
        philosophical from taproots soaked in breath

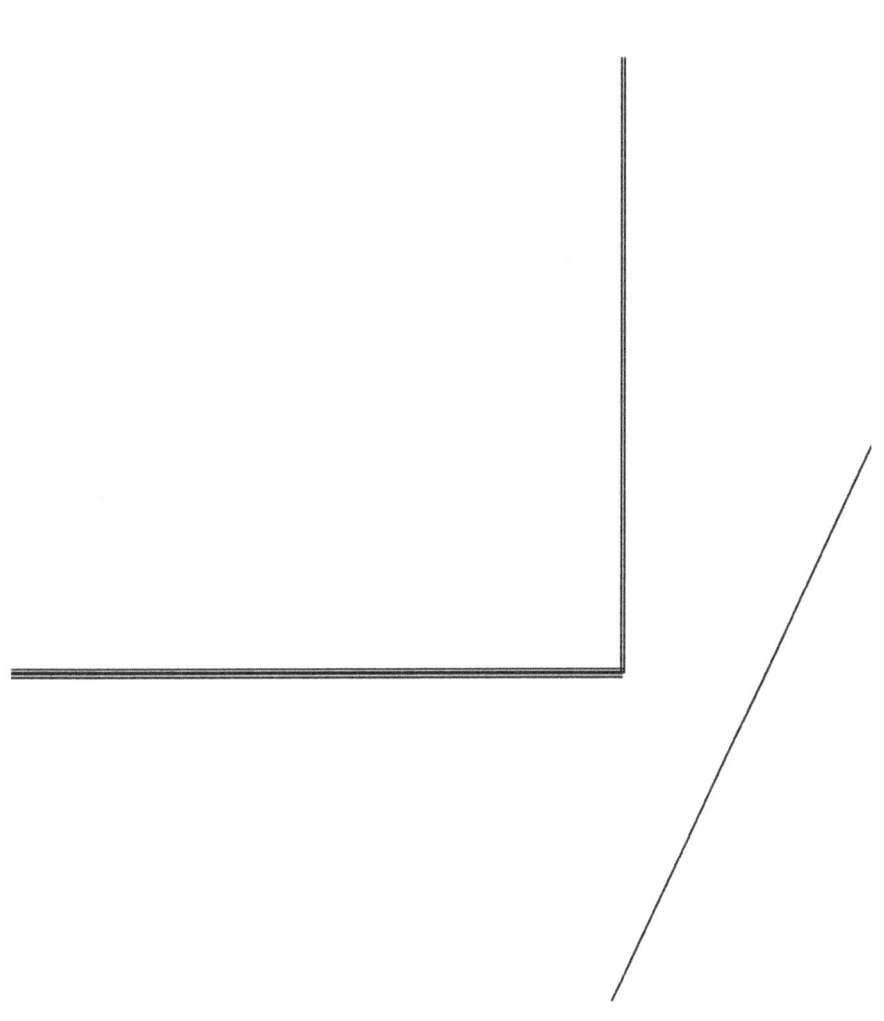

THIRTY-ONE QUESTIONS TO ASK YOURSELF WHILE LOOKING IN A MIRROR

How did you learn to grow hair on your body?

Did you know that within your body you will have all the experience of heaven and/or hell that you will ever have?

How is it that your body, which is both known and unknown to you, embodies the Unknown, so that alchemists, theologians, mystics, scientists, skeptics, psychologists, and you yourself have peered, will peer, for millennia ad perpetuum into your body to discover the mystery of creation, or simply to know the complex fact of existence?

When did you decide to invent language?

When you sleep, how do bodily sensations become mental images, narratives even, long strings of absurd vignettes?

Why don't you laugh in your sleep?[1] Why do you laugh?

Why has your body made so many errors relative to your judgment of it, a judgment which, like heaven and/or hell occurs only in your body, and which may be the only judgment or the only judge you will ever know?

When you ever feared that you might go mad, was it your body's fear? What did your body do about it?

If you are not the same you you were ten years ago, is your body the same body it was ten years ago?

You have had the sensation of dying and awakening to new life a thousand times; has your body done the same? in synchrony with you, or in a rhythm of its own?

Why is your body so complex?

What is the relationship between the organelles in the cells of your thigh and the organelles in the cells of your brain?[2]

Are there decisions your body has made which you haven't yet accepted? Of all the sensations your body receives, how do you, or your body, decide which will be pain, which will be beauty?

Why can't you fly?

Why did you invent language?

What occurs in your body which is never dictated by thought, not exercised by the control of reason, exempt from all aesthetic or moral concern?

When did you begin to achieve the balance necessary between the chemical/biological/muscular/neural/cellular processes of your body and what is so often called the external world of other bodies, including distant influences such as moons or other universes.[3]

Reminder: Ask these questions while looking in a mirror, a full length mirror (invented in the 1st Century AD), if possible; naked is best.

Does your mind lead your body, or vice versa? Or neither? Or both?

UNNAMED: The Emotions

What cognitive abilities or speed did you give up along the evolutionary way to make brain-space available for language? Was (is) it worth the trade-off?

Do you believe that your senses: sight (smell) sound (touch) smell (sight) taste (smell) touch (sight) function solely to promote the ongoing life of your body, or do they have other purposes?

How similar in detail — eyes (stature) teeth (spine) feet (immune system) hands (brain) — is your body to the bodies of your ancestors when they lived in the mouths of caves?

How do the chemical reactions, the electrical charges cross what appear to be those chasms that exist within your body to become consciousness, image, dream, thought, language, memory, writing, reading?

How did your mouth learn to shape all the sounds it needs to speak? Is that what it was made for? How many words has your mouth spoken in your lifetime? How many has it refrained from speaking?

Can you ask the question: "Was your mouth made for speaking?" without implying intention?

Why do you cry? What happens in your body when you cry? Are humans the only creatures who cry? Can your body remember when it has cried? Did it need to learn to cry?

Does your body have a rational explanation for its being?[4]

How does your body understand each of these terms: fear.

Martin Nakell

        dejection.

            love.

                sensuality.

injustice.

        clarity.   action.

        confusion.   wealth?

Of all the passions your body owns which most fully express desire and what is desire and when desire is fulfilled what remains?

Command your body to a voluntary movement: raise your arm, lift your leg, talk, smile: by what neurological activity by what translation of thought back across those chasms can you feel your muscles respond to your consciousness?1

Look at your body, what a neutral thing it is, in itself. Heart, blood, oxygen, movement, pulsation, chemistry, electricity, water, cells, brain cells, dna, all of a universe, no more no less than a sun itself, or some star at the edge of your universe, the beginning of the middle of the end of certainty and

unknowing in each atom of each colliding subatom, all neutral in itself. What is it you have done with this neutral material what structures what works of days in hours what paradisos in passing wrecks abandoned charred remains doors leaped chasm exits followed by entrance into what is it you have done that has brought you here to this mirror now it/self of sand silver light carried light to be looking at your body to be posing a spontaneous interrogation whose answers abide at the precise point of their originlessness within the narrator of your question?

UNNAMED: The Emotions

The early evolutionists still believed that an internal mechanism drove your body to a pinnacle of developmental perfection. You, who accept your body as a transitory moment in a field of everlasting change (yet understanding that it took half a million years to develop the eye) how well has your body adapted to its present conditions?

What does your body think of the following concepts: irony.

        a definitive enigma.

                an excess of metaphysics.

                      metamorphosis.

interrogation?

---

1 Always turned towards creation, we see/only a mirroring of the free/ dimmed by our breath
    —Rilke, *Eighth Duino Elegy*

2 through laughing anointments through annotations the reversals of mirrors
    —Alexander Batshteyn, *The Configurations*, 1877

3 trails forgetfulness/among blessings uttered/with temporary refusals to look/mirrors
    —Fr. Samuel Konnekhey, X: *Notes to the Book of Hours*, 1436

4 Mr Power watches "Long John Fanning ascend toward Long John Fanning in the mirror," but isn't deceived by circumstances.
    —Stuart Gilbert, James Joyce's Ulysses, a Study, 1930

Martin Nakell

BEGIN ASCENT OF THE UNIVERSAL HUMANKIND

You awake in the Beautiful City.

The body is an instrument of knowing.

Together, you walk up the steps to the Temple. As you get closer to the two doors, open, the last two steps steepen, so steep they dwarf you so steep you build ladders to lean against them but you can't build any ladder tall enough and the distance grows until the opening at the Temple doors once so obvious is now absurd. Is this where you build? What are you building? And what does it mean when you accept the post of Mayor of the Beautiful City?

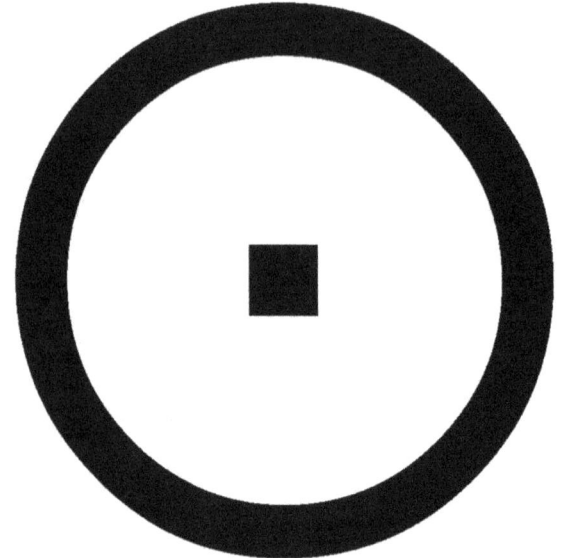

Martin Nakell

FURTHER ADVENTURES AD ISCHIA

That there is no inertia in the universal chaos or in the internal order of things

That to eat a local dish, say, insalata caprese in Italy south of Rome, is to realize how tradition over hundreds of years produces a realization which explores certain absolute realities of white, red, green which separates the contradictions of milk from seedflesh from leaf while insisting that milk seedflesh leaf converge under the stonesilentarid treesunborne aegis of olive oil in an ordering of chaos that is at once seasonal, perpetual, turbulent, determinant, celebratory, indulgent, personal as interpersonal, individual as collective, singular as repetitive, symbolic as actual, charming as serious, partaking of the past as of the future as they commingle within the multilayered dimension of the present as the post-Einsteinium physics of time and the 10,000 year old agronomy of agriculture converge in the act of life on earth

That the news – always a momentary phenomena – arrives today printed on papyrus sheets that announce the current veracity quotient of prophecy the arrival and departure of ships the odds for and against contracting and recovering from given diseases the economic and the dynamic cost of converting chaos into order, order into revelation, revelation into society, society into meaning, meaning into speech, speech into sun, sun into water, water into ink, ink into wine, wine into shoes, shoes into symbols for shoes and the difference in the market price for shoes from yesterday to today.

That today on the one day everyone in the city and on its neighboring island awake at the same moment everyone, sensing something is up, lay in their beds to listen to the ambient sound which consist mostly of lizardsong so that later everyone in the city and on its neighboring island remember at some point throughout the day the common idea that hearing a lizard's song heightens an awareness of the silence into which that lizard sings making that silence also a kind of song in

counterpoint to the lizardsong yet throughout the day that silence is occupied by the business of living even though if one listens one still hears the lizardsong now as backdrop. All of which causes one of these persons to wonder about the relationship of foreground to background of him or herself in particular in relation to his/her speech and silence and in relation to all those he/she knows in the relationship of him/herself to history in relationship to her or his work in relationship to the idea of meaning in relationship to the local economy to the always unfair sometimes brutal organization of social structure and class to the lizard itself that is was she/he foreground and the lizard's singing background or was there no such thing as foreground background but only ground the stage of a universal theater on which everything including the lizards lay out their loyalty to time which are bodies in motion within bodies in motion as she/he concluded, either chaos in search of order or order in search of further order which is both song and beast or the eye opening with waking closing with sleep.

That years ago emerging from her sleep going out into a world he had looked at her that he is still looking. That she said something to him then without speaking that she is still talking to him. That in the intervening years she had come to distinguish between form and phantom but what has he distinguished he will continue to look at someone as the many masks that he sees wherever he looks the plethora of masquerade but in particular in the piazza of the History of Speech filled with the unnumbered faces of the thousands of lives lighten the word he told her. Then fill it with helium. If you are stuck at a crossroads he told her years before go only after the sun sets, only at night but return to an origin only in daylight. He looked at her then as if to say look! we will continue to save each other only when necessary. Now he says something different involving a theology of the objective world. After murder, they will seek redemption.

After communion, they all tell someone else the truth they reserve for their own nightmares. Clinging to life air breathes air. Rocks enter the landscape without any notion of error. We invent the gesture in our void as a mark of our genius, he told her. His eyes, she can't quite read his eyes which doesn't stop her from learning his alphabet. Sheinvents forms of recreation as methods of contemplation which open her to chaos. She brings back her souvenirs. She arranges them in shifting orders of significance. She gives credence to a stranger crossing a street who glances back at her over and again over because he is an agriculture, a god, a projection, a cry in the street. What's up? What's up?

That power cannot come down only from the barrel of an historical surrealism. That, conquered during the war, we preserved our absurdity. That no one not even the dead enemy is excluded from the conversation at the table with all the rights of an opinion and communion. That we awoke at dawn to the cock-crow but slept into the arms of that day. Water everywhere, water, water. We drink. That sneaking behind the enemy lines we destroy the watchtower to take visual command of the beasts of the bay raising our glasses to victory imbibing beast, bay, historical surrealism. We have outwitnessed by the device of osmosis the daemon Chaos who appears at our table as the guest, Order.

TO CROSS

The purpose of a sea journey is the sea let's not kid around with it but why not and why not now right now? The poem couldn't go on even thoughting wants to it.

Martin Nakell

ALIVES FORWARD TOWARD THE UNIVERSAL HUMANKIND

you to have forgotten a childhood completely whether your own or someone's. it didn't happen that you fled from the side of a rowboat the bees flying faceward. neither did it happen that you awoke in the back seat of a locked car alone then tumbled your way in to the strange house, and safety. neither did it happen that you stood with your feet in the lake gazing at water at lapping at sound at nearness at pleasure at love. no, it did not happen that you walked a winter-slogged sidewalk hunter's handwarmer in hand becoming a man. it never took place that your father surprised you in the bath saying you're growing hair down there good for you. you never saw the neighbor girl kneeling by the altar she had made of fall leaves. you never saw that. you didn't hear the cantor intone the resonance of history. you never became a jew or catholic or buddhist or jain or muslim or sikh. you did not see the desire of your father for your mother suddenly waken his visage. you did not watch the summer end; nor the spring begin. you did not write the poem. you did not wake up at night with the need to write the poem. you did not hear the words form into families of words. you did not sell your birthright. you did not go out with your father to light fires in the four corners of the fields. you did not apply salves to wounds. you did not kiss a night. you did not whisper to yourself nor did you whisper to him or to her. and because you did not do any of these things, because you don't remember being the one who did any of these things, because you cannot have the consciousness of the one who did any of these things, you do all and every one of them and more, more, much more, now, at this moment, in the ever continuous moment at the road called Contiuums by the monument called Singularities.

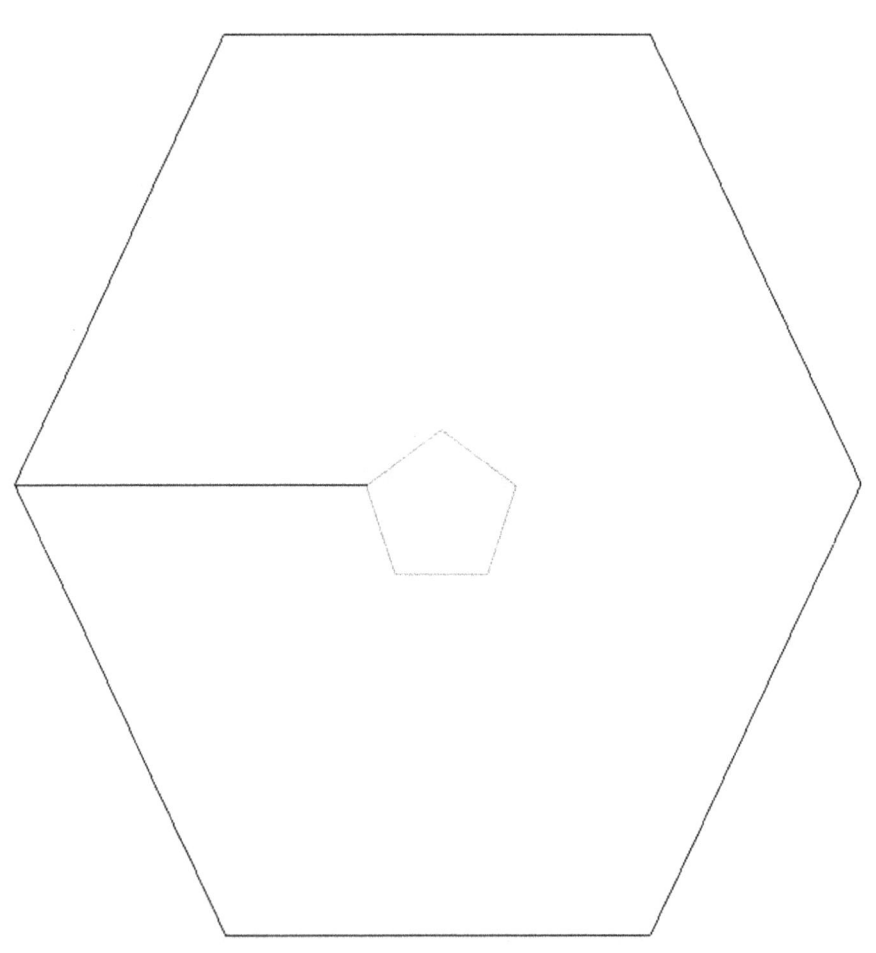

Martin Nakell

FROM A STUDY ON THE HISTORY OF LANGUAGES

Here they are my words entangled with your letters they cannot escape even into the countryside!

CON:VERSE

when he gno that light come from he kno language do grow on tree – or izzzit sea - he touch that one also is form within formz he see he nu was have to wait to know first thing if

he breath he breathe inhale he a word first if is its opposition dissolve in solution he take action for clothing he make life from by blow on her over moistiest tongue she arrive wild she uncontrollable daemon shehe if you please she molecule by at atom fragment at grain by she him blood be bonehim he big be like with child be he with tree – or izzit sea if by roiling byin sea bottomlessextantextentbroadsentcenter sea

brick stone glass cloth wool cotton history personal history family history country history the history of time including the a'fore tha Bang, Big, wherein the odors of brick stone glass cloth wool cotton like he odor of cow dung from a barn coincide with sight gnoledge that lightdark come form if is togather izzzzzzzz

Martin Nakell

AT NIGHT IZZZZ DAWN IZ

Sleeping birds fill all the beds
Sleeping, birds fill the beds
The beds are filled by all the sleeping
sleeping fills
            Birds are filling
Filling. Birds. Fallow far are sleep the birds
Birdbody by birdbody in the crook or
nook or nich or crick or crack as
bend of body bird flight asleep but not
in a bodymind of birdbody just sleep
and flighting are two things being
never together ever riven by
human kiss tongue spittle air breath bliss
gone over to the bird side riverdrawn
down waterslid be there at the one
human beings asleep sleeping all the purpose in the
earthaverse crossing all the riverrilling waterstorms
tossing

tongue in abation pawned to purchase bedside place among them , sleeping, birds and birds filling all the sleepest air that human's body birdside need to be covered by airbird only the birds have songbird dalliance before a songbird burst expected but by know one except percept of explorer bird asleep among amidst awith awidth a well along the huss breath of all the filling bed birds in one uni son into earthever to dissolve a silence sliced in two or three or four or five, alive. still. sleep. bird.

UNNAMED: The Emotions

TO ZLEEP OF THE UNIVERSAL HUMANKIND

To have dreamt that you were asleep outdoors under a canopy of dried grasses. Or to have dreamt that you had fallen asleep on a bench outside the engine repair shop where you work, all the others still working inside, behind you. Or to have dreamt that you were in a session of psychoanalysis with Sigmund Freud where you fell asleep on his couch to have dreamt that when you awoke Dr Freud interpreted your dream without your having yet spoken a word. Or to have dreamt that you fell asleep in a field out in the countryside where.where you'd been walking, then wake up to find yourself surrounded by grass-feeding space-staring shifting from cow-hoof to cow-hoof the wind a cow wind. Or to have dreamt that you fell asleep floating on a rubber raft seawide the clouds above ripples with wind in the same windrippled pattern that the sand on the sea-floor below you ripples in precisely the same patterns by the motion of water. Or perhaps you dreamt that you fell asleep as a child, awakened by your sister, laughing to herself, tickling the soles of your feet with a feather. Or you dreamt that you fell asleep on top of a tall building, rolled over the edge to fly at will through the city, in and around the buildings good and evil, over houses awakened, with flocks of indifferent birds. Or perhaps you dreamt that you fell asleep for so long that when you awoke you found yourself in a future so brilliantly advanced that you flew beside a light beam. Or did you sleep, dreaming you were a flower among a field of flowers invaded by a swarm of bees who drank themselves into a stupor is ecstasy on the juices made over the year. Or did you sleep to awaken frightened not knowing of what but with a need so strong to fight flight that you lay frozen but could not unfreeze yourself for several years. Or did you sleep to dream that you were being born just then emerging into the mystery of living from the mystery of the womb suckling the thumb of your right hand you prepared yourself to say, "Well now ain't that just something I mean ain't this the cat's miou I mean hot-damn Momma hot Po;;a damn will you just look at all this there's daylight nightlight apples and all these golden elephants!" Or did you fall asleep dreaming that you wrote and kept writing as you filled up pages of paper new empty white linen pages appearing sewn together in a line of pages that extend back becoming bark then stone as far as the origin of scripture. Or did you sleep to dream that you had wakened actually before you slept in an enigma explained by a series of chemical formulas that described also how to make gold of base metal and prayers the names to be used in curses. Or did you sleep in your own bed beside your own mate to awaken in an embrace in which you had switched bodies one with the other but it was alright because before arising to coffee with fruit your bodies switched back again into the forms you were always used to whatever they are.

A

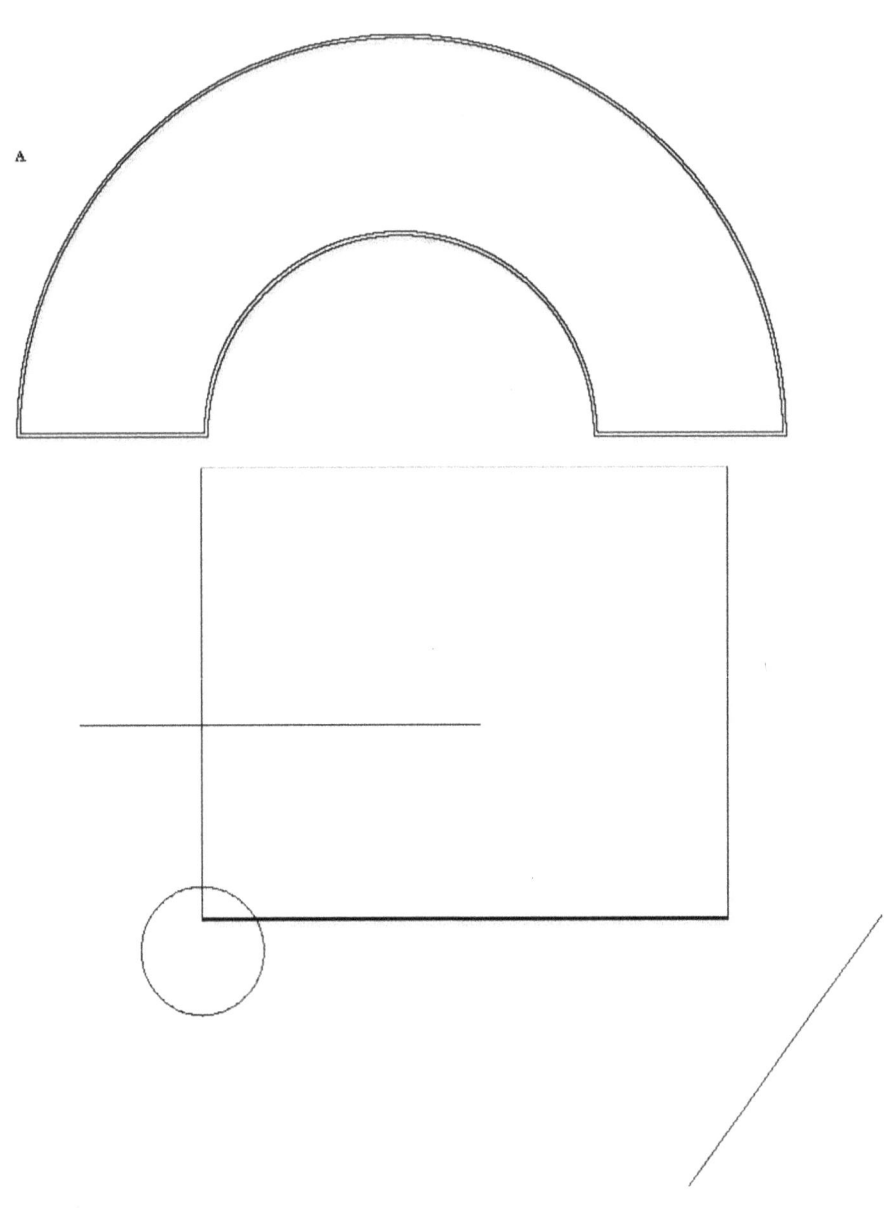

THE REPETITIONS

The open hand with the air past unties a world unraveling a space conditioned by presence

The unclasped hand and the two sets of five fingers still as the number ten unwavering the wind stiff as calm

Reminiscences of hands, open or clasped together or around, holding, say, a pen, or a gallon of water

The tree in its light and dark and wooded greens sits in the open field across which the finger points looking for where hay had been stacked

The open hand reminiscent of an oath but not an oath but the oath reminiscent of strength a covenant

written and re-written over so much time that it has become not an ur-text but commentary,

steadfast in ingathering

A CONCRETE

always it becomes

and too,

        never too
        late

   & light

        & a window

            becomes one who only

                  loves

        the face across the table
        talking

    the plate
    the hum

        of a computer

            still:voice:whose:

what is never heard

in leaving	in remains
in allowance	in forbearance
in freedom	in, slowly, cessation
in blessing	in transition
in departure	fade out fade
in escape	allow in
	desertion in
	continuum

a choice where there
is

      no middle

Martin Nakell

                    a via negativa a
                                  via innamorata perhaps isa

a street
cobbled

     & a hot sun

   he will to have
   a lemonade
   he will to sit
   in the battlefield abandoned

he will cough up
the history of mysteries solved

               plays with you

                        or plays you

                                    they cajole

and then all this

        black

                will be orange

    a speech

          a will

                intervene

                        a sun

   a warm

         a sun

something between was
        or ancome

UNNAMED: The Emotions

as, at

    the
    greatest
    a
    triumph
    ambiguity
    from
    each
    word
    work hard all day long

Martin Nakell

AGRIBIZ

the act of science invents a space between atoms where language might utter its certain truths

. . . . ever knows . . . . . whether to look backward or forward for inspiration vibrates in the space opened between breaths of the animal Sun while the lover sleeps the avatar washes sin into a river of light scrubs guilt until it is free of its promise then ,, only then does the lightness herself illuminate to burst forth when the seed opens but the time is ripe for picking so make hay hay make while the glows moon for the old gods await you in the furrows where the witches have buried the fox come home home come to your supper laughter to good friends astride the wind that unties them

can poetry be that art that never was that always will ancome

can poetry be that art that stays in the room when everyone else leaves it to await their return can poetry be the only artform that cannot be translated into words

ICE CREAM

An event at Sperlunga

A day in the sea

There was a god there oncet upon the back of the swift horse

where a woman they call the –goddess diaphanous– now named rails

how she rallies at frolics

in the ancome

The first law of the epicures who flew in from the east

is that life is pain

or bread

how the first obedient child whispers at her mother's knee

her voice in air foreshortened by the sound of engines driving

from the west some message-bearing

some to reach the event at Sperlunga before its sun rests

Disorder again captures the people in a turbulence of forgetfulness

if only form were new again take the word cup for example then drink from it if you would start out on a commonholy trail oh meaning vibrate as a word eve such as cup or puc a humble thing where onct no god had ever dwelt upon a rainy day

FRAGMENTATION

each 1 a poem

———————————————

each bit of food floats
to the mouth
something not spoken of
doesn't exist
equal weight is equal time.

———————————————

"I have imagined this. You
go find it. Bring it back to me. I'll give it to you.

———————————————

"I myself am a reversal of
expectations. I followed someone
who led me into a vibrant city of poverty
where the poor whirl &
a wind whistles.

———————————————

The endless possibilities of stories
that are inherent in things in places preserve
them

———————————————

when you know the
language you lose something without
the translation

———————————————

UNNAMED: The Emotions

PANDOLCE WITH THE UNIVERSAL HUMANKIND

When he lost all his identities at the breakfast table he discovered that laughter is the act of nihilism clearing the world of old hierarchs. When he took up a book called Hope he read it from cover to cover to cover to cover and kept reading into the sound where he knew the seed resounded. When they asked him if he believed in the system he told them to be bold to imagine that there is no system then to let it appear. When they charged him a hundred twenty-six dollars for lunch he refused to vote in the upcoming election. When it came time to celebrate the gone poet he gathered with everyone who had learned to read from the inside out because they are the ones who know that meaning is no more absent from the atom than it is from that art. Someone at the festival declared above the din that for the gone poet to write a poem was a form of ejaculation meaning that love plays a part in the order of the universal even where eros crosses the bridge called suspension to reach the either called thou. all this requires a disciplined mind so used to travel that it calls on the body for help in achieving recognition of the sphere of influence which is its natural due and with which it plays its dues in nature. When he discovered electricity he declared it had been there all along just like the other mysteries left to reveal. Gathering the buildings from downtown the skyscrapers the restaurants the lofts the city hall the churches he melted them into a poem which he read aloud at the corner of Him and Her attracting all the City's attention. When he went to hell he never went alone and when he went to heaven he took everyone each thing along and when he stayed put he traveled always by bicycle the most common form of transport worldwide outside of walking because that includes the animal world although wind comes in a close second and perhaps first carrying as it does. When he read the Special Theory of Relativity he wrote to his closest friend a physicist calling it a description of his mind his friend the physicist responded by telegram asking him what about your soul. He responded by joining The Church of the Theory of Special Relativity for the 21st Century where he achieved Special Enlightenment twice before twice arresting in the arms of chance. When he said Come they came when he said Go they went.

MINERAL CHEMICAL ARITHMETICAL HUMANKIND

WHAT ARE CLOUDS

because the world is new it was just born yesterday we don't yet know how to use it
we don't know how to make flags or clean windows we don't know how to give birth to our young
we have to learn how to cross the street safely we have to learn how to kiss and whom
and how much and for how long
we have to learn how to sleep now and we have to learn where to go to learn how to sleep we have so much to do and we're tired
we have to learn how to use a door how to open how to close and whereinto/ wherefrom
we have to learn to use our mouths to speak to say nothing of our bodies to move to the music
yet how do we make music or an instrument how do we discover that
we have the problem of a thousand possible errors ahead of us
we can name the colors but why would we do that why not leave them alone
we can invent all of the languages choosing any one for any particular need at any given time
how do we use arithmetics to our advantage what can we discover what can we not calculate
how do we grow vegetables how do we carry flowers to a friend
how do we love a mother a father how do we treat them
where can we go to learn to pack a lunch to find out how to take a political or a sociological survey
we have to learn to distinguish between all the races that sprang up all at once yesterday but why who knows

UNNAMED: The Emotions

because there are things we can refuse to learn even as there are things we cannot refuse to learn
and we must musn't we learn to diet to lose weight and to go to church if we want some solace
or some of that kind of joy if we learn that it's good for us
we have to learn how to falsify and to hide from each other we have so much to learn!
we have to learn how to invest in the stock market how to breathe
don't we have to learn how and whom and when to hate and what is hatred and how does it feel on the blood in the mind
how do we undue the damage that nature does to nature how can we learn to do that
how do we ever get any revenge
of course we have to learn to read an art which takes a lifetime to develop
we will have to learn things that will enslave us we will have to
how do we learn to what group we belong
how to we learn to free ourselves from every group
and then to return if we want to
how can we learn from whom where how to meditate and how far to go with this
we better learn how to fight
do we already know how to pick fruit from a fruit tree
do we already know how to wash ourselves
do we know how to climb into and out of caves
what did we come here knowing? yesterday. just yesterday.
it seems a million years ago but at the same time it seems just yesterday just now.
when will it come time to differentiate good from evil. are we up to that task.
how will we learn truth from lies. is it possible we'll sometimes not be sure at all.
how do we learn to go too far.
how do we learn to see into nature into the skies into the cells of own skin and how long will that take us

WHAT IS GRASS

How many Americans believe in Heaven and Hell? How many French?
When Germany comes to dominate Europe again will the same danger revive in her ambitions?
Is America the world's newest Empire or is it a democratic influence around the world?
Have you the patience to read each line of this poem to contemplate to consider it?
What constitutes sexual deviation?
Does the belief in a natural unashamed unabashed "primitive" or "tribal" sexuality represent a reality or a myth?
Is language unnatural?
Is language ineffective?
What do we ask of language?
Why is the little girl in the backyard next door screaming?
Why is the wife in the apartment next door screaming?
Do animals scream?
What can we intuit of animal life? What can we know/understand/experience/feel of it? From the life of a caterpillar to the life of a hawk to the life of an aardvark?
Is a college education a gateway to a successful life and career?
Is college life a sexual madhouse?
Do you remember every sexual encounter of your life?
Do you remember those encounters with pleasure or with regret?
Do you remember some of those encounters with a mixture of pleasure and regret?
Are you afraid of dying?
Do you want to live long enough to accomplish your goals?
Are your goals moral or immoral? Can you tell the difference?
Are you alienated from your family? Why?
Did your mother give you sufficient love and support?

UNNAMED: The Emotions

Do you miss the patriotic fervor that past generations seem to have enjoyed?
Do you belong?
Have you been able in your life to bring your head and your heart and your breath into harmony or are they at war with each other?
Did your father give you sufficient love and support?
What is wholeness either your own or the wholeness of the universe?
Is there a wholeness to Time?
If you could change one seemingly unchangeable thing about yourself which trait would it be?
If you could actively preserve one seemingly unchangeable thing about yourself which trait would it be?
If you could change one seemingly unchangeable thing about the world which fact would it be?
Does absence make the heart grow fonder or forgetful?
For what are you nostalgic? Are you nostalgic for the present?
What so far unquenchable desire propels you?
Do you like books or movies?
Have you ever committed a sexually deviant act? How was it? Are you ashamed?
Do you believe in the power of beauty to save you? On a daily basis?
What do you do with your cruelty?

WHAT IS STONE

I went to the market
to get oranges
but I was attacked
on the way
and nearly murdered.
What if I had been

murdered?
I went to the circus
to see all the animal acts
so I could understand better
my own mind.
I went to the aquarium
where I saw the dolphins
press up against the vast glass
where the gathering of children pressed
their own faces
so that I understood the child's mind.
I went to hell and back.
I went to the past and I went to the future.
They were utterly different but I was not.
I went to Zanzibar I went to Ultima Thule
I went to Disneyland I went to Aliceinwonderland
I went to Dead Sea because it is the Dead Sea
because I had to see such a phenomena although
neither in Hebrew nor in Arabic is it called the Dead Sea
I went to the top of Mount Zion
to see the face of God
I went to the top of Mt. Olympus
so that Zeus would teach me how
gods copulate with humans
how it is for the gods how it is for the humans
I went to the White House
I went to Nirvana and begged not to be sent home
I went to the end of my mind I found what I found there
I went to the end of your mind to find the mind of my reader
I went to the act of going to discover a useless philosophy that I loved
I went to the opium den to lead my brothers and my sisters out of the desert

UNNAMED: The Emotions

WHAT IS A SEA

when you transplant don't water the plant right away give it time to recover from transplant shock
an army doesn't march on its stomach it marches on its will to fight which depends on the need for war
if you loved me you would help me in my distress although a dog may love you it will flee your emotional outcries in fear
when it rains cats and dogs run inside
if global climate change is what they say it is we are truly not long for this planet
when you love everything living that you can see right now you have achieved an incredible state of bliss
if you hate me I want to know why but I may not be able to do anything about it
when the birds are singing like crazy you can't get up you can't just walk away
if a hive of bees goes wild goes so mad with the ecstasy of feeding in a field of lavender
that you can walk among them unharmed you can partake of the ecstasy not of feeding but of being in that kind of display of nature's precisely honed passions
when you say that bees go mad with ecstasy you attribute human feelings to the animal world but who's to say that ecstasy is human or only human that is that we invented it most likely we didn't
if you suffer a terrible disease from which you recover you will never be the same some
say they now will never forget to be present in their lives but that's not all there is to it
when the wind blows stand still in it see what it does to you
if you kiss your beloved and s/he responds only with his/her daily fatigue don't withdraw into fantasy this is your life
when your mother scolded you as a child remember how you were were you frightened
or angry or defensively bemused or ashamed or guilty feeling

if you carry those associations with you as memory you are trapped forever in stupidity
when your mother and father fight ferociously as they may stay the hell out of it it's not your fault
and it's not your business
if you discover that your best friend has been sleeping with your wife/husband you might lose
faith in yourself or in life itself and become evermore bitter but there are more important dangers
to bitterness for you to face along the way
when you see your wife/husband and it makes you rejoice then rejoice with all your might even
though that might could be a quiet but consuming energy in your body and a passing moment
if you walk into the room where the executive committee is meeting and the issue is one of life
or death always choose life no matter what the consequences this is not the law but it is the only
thing that you might cherish at the end of the day
when the sun shines don't make hay make whoopee for christ sake
if the sun shines so strongly for so long that it wipes out your crops
make a mock King out of straw, cut it into four, plant it in the four corners of your field for next year's abundance even if you don't believe it
when technology overruns your life overwhelms it drives you insane remember the invention of the
wheel the invention of gunpowder the invention of the salk vaccine and be comforted, human
if to be human seems small and insignificant don't wait for anything to contradict that
it's ok it's truly ok
when the president of your country betrays you tell everyone you expected no better

UNNAMED: The Emotions

if all politicians are crooks then aren't all men/women crooks
when you were an infant in diapers even a child in jumpers
you did not in your wildest moment imagine
you would come to where you are now
if you know where you are now turn around three times utter
an incantation as old as you know of one announce
your arrival in a formal declaration forget about change it's nothing
important to know about
when you're broke and the kids ask you for money there's no way to explain it
because it's about the mystery called money and the unforgiving
disappointments
of a sorrow based in communion and betrayal which is really a joke of the
mysterious kind to laugh at
if you had to choose between peace and prosperity you would find that the
choice has to be obvious
when the saints come marching in it's just possible you will be there
if the news in the newspaper no matter how bad somehow we find that
everyone adjusts
when you sit somewhere in what we call silence somehow we always find we are
hearing things
if you sit somewhere in silence often what you hear can be very pleasant and
cause an awareness of heightened sensation
when we eat carefully we can have the same sensation of heightened awareness
if we plan out our lives very carefully we find that some people realize those
plans while
others find they have so changed they do not even recognize their original
plans as
having been made by themselves and that this can be shocking if exciting
when most people run out of money because of some personal or national
economic failure they somehow adjust
if you want something just take it
when you look at the work of a great painter or artist it may be difficult if

impossible to articulate
your response but it's also unnecessary
if a celebration takes place honoring someone you know you may find that by joining in you are yourself celebrated
when a revolution takes place anything could happen it's all wide open but we have to wonder if
the past can change all that much
if we apply enough of a force – any force – gravitational, electrical, magnetic, mechanical, heat, cold –
to any system it will set that system into a revolution of its entire nature

WHAT IS HUMAN

after leaving new york she found that over the next few years she left it more and more and more
after having a strange dream of complete and lifelong redemption w/no source but his own psyche
the ex-soldier did not weep at the breakfast table the way he feared that he would but he calmly told
his wife and his children and they wept for him or for themselves
after completing her master's degree in creative writing she found herself free to write how she had
always wanted to write but had always feared would be unacceptable after the deluge
after initiating the divorce he lived off of fury for many months but then it became only a sorrow
that gnawed at him daily dragging him down
after the war in Vietnam – many years later – he returned to where he had served as a nurse not
for his own sake but to honor those whose lives he could not save. not only the

village but a senior
Vietnamese military officer greeted him warmly then he couldn't understand human life how it could
unravel so
after discovering that speech contains silence and silence contains speech he now feared
neither silence nor speech
after sitting on the stairs late at night listening to the adults' party in progress he went back
to his room to compose the first symphony – a short eight minutes – of his life. he would
occasionally conduct it as an opening shot to concerts around the world. it made him smile and it put him in the groove
after years of fighting through the court system the civil rights case lost at the top how could such injustice prevail?
after giving up on a career in law she started a home in Mexico for abused children which
she ran for 42 years after which she turned it over to one of the children who had stayed on with her
after abandoning his faith the ex-priest entered a life of indulgence and debauchery from
which he never reformed, of which he never repented, to which he dedicated himself
with a religious fervor from which he drew inspiration
after going to the museum to see her own exhibit the artist remarked to her friend
that she had never realized how moving how powerful how successful the third painting in the now-famous series of five actually was how she herself was affected by it
after he lost his small business in the recession and floundered even into bankruptcy
he was unnerved by thoughts of suicide but heartened to see that equally

powerful feelings
of anger and love also rose
after the secretary of defense retired he revealed that every night for the last
four years of war
he wept for the wounded and fallen his orders had sent into battle
after the fall of mankind and the expulsion from the garden of eden a host of
amazing
things occurred including the birth of human will and the triumph of the spirit
and the appearance of sorcerers and the reflections in water and the migrations
of birds and the huge variety of colors of flowers and the glimpses mankind
would cherish into the real paradise of being
after the religious court sentenced the dog to stoning for its evil transgressions
against the holy spirit the state intervened with its laws against cruelty to
animals but it was too late the stoning had occurred and everyone
in the religious community denied that it happened and the body
of the dog was nowhere to be found
after the interracial marriage broke the boundaries of custom and law
and fear each of the races lost its sexual fantasies about the other
after the man in the golden hat told the greatest joke ever told
so many people came close to dying of laughter-asphyxiation
that he reserved that telling only for those who could take it:
either the laughter or the dying
after the song came the music after the music came the singing
after the singing came the chanting after the chanting came
the humming after the humming came the speaking after
the speaking came the oration after the oration came the
applause after the applause came the call for encore encore
and after the call for encore encore came more came more
after the lifting of the siege of the city came a huge dance
of victory in the main square that lasted for as long
as anyone could keep breathing that is until now
and beyond now

UNNAMED: The Emotions

after the death of her grandmother came the
creative fury that sustained her work for years to come
after his bar mitzvah at 13 he already feared there would
be nothing more to live for no great height to ascend
after sex when they lay in bed the visions passing unimpeded
through their minds without fear or anticipation or desire
they swore they would not re-enter the world of linear time
of spatial orientation ever again even if hunger drove them
after the death of the last descendent of the turbulent family
a family friend draped a white cloth over the void left behind
after the crow swept in to take its fill the smaller
birds with the littler beaks took their turn
that's how it works
and that's how it is
after midnight one night everyone noticed there was
actually an untimed space until 1:000000001∞ began
of course everyone wanted it to last forever so they could see
into it clearly to their amusement
after the invention of the telescope the eye would
never be the same and the eye is a muscle of the brain
and the brain is the seat of the human soul
as first observed as first confirmed through a telescope
after the city fell to the siege the people wandering
into exile wrote poems of exquisite sorrow they composed
songs of lament borrowing on melodies from long ago
and later that would become the blues
after – even vicious, barbaric even – struggles they never
anticipated they were able to build their spacious, airy homes
which flowed into the outside and back into and through the inside
of these actual structures
after Ahab – in another version of the myth coming from another village –
gave up his rage against Moby Dick, Ahab sailed home, vowing openly

to the crew whose lives he thus saved, that he, and they, would find
meaning and miracle in everyday ordinary life but the myth stops there;
we don't know of his successes or failures thereafter
after losing 16 pounds quickly the last 4 pounds were very hard to get off
after spending a night with the obnoxious couple he woke up ready to
argue with his wife but instead argued with life itself until he could find it
funny
as long as he didn't have to see them again but knew that he would
after the air conditioning went on life in the desert became tolerable again
if of course artificial feeling and a cop-out on the truth of the desert after the
contractor finished that
building the apex of his – as he called it –
artist-contractor's – career he did not fall into the despair that he feared
the satisfaction never ended
after years of struggling with money they knew very well that money would not
buy them happiness
after all the medical remedies failed, after all the doctors gave up, she healed
and the doctors called it the placebo effect but a placebo of what they could not
say after leaving prison he called himself a Jew in the Wilderness who now had
his Time
of Wandering to do
after the assassination of Martin Luther King every major city
in America named a boulevard after him that traveled
through the cities' African-American neighborhoods often
cutting a swath of poverty & culture onto the new map
after studying the history of science and taking a degree
in contemporary poetry he co-founded the Institute for the Harmony
of Science and Poetics with Headquarters in Los Angeles and Tokyo

WHAT ARE MINERALS

A mineral is a naturally occurring solid chemical substance that is formed through biogeochemical processes and that has a characteristic chemical composition, a highly ordered atomic structure, and specific physical properties

WHAT ARE CHEMICALS

He read the story of his father as it was written in the history books it wasn't the man he knew leaving him on the brink of a void he knew he would never need to fill

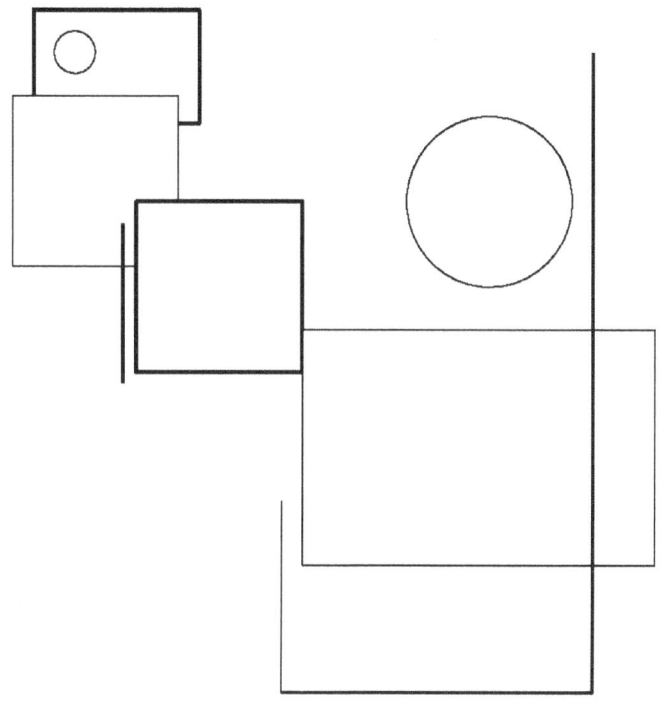

www.ingramcontent.com/pod-product-compliance
Lightning Source LLC
Chambersburg PA
CBHW022115090426

42743CB00008B/865